D0946797

JEFF GORDON:
Simply the Best

BY JIM GIGLIOTTI

TRADITION BOOKS™
EXCELSIOR, MINNESOTA

Published by **Tradition Books**™ and distributed to the
school and library market by **The Child's World**®
P.O. Box 326
Chanhassen, MN 55317-0326
800/599-READ
http://www.childsworld.com

Photo Credits
Cover and title page: Jonathan Ferrey/Getty Images (left);
  Sports Gallery/Brian Spurlock (right)
Allsport: 13; 17 (David Taylor); 28; 30 (Jamie Squires)
Sports Gallery: 3, 20, 24 (Al Messerschmidt); 4, 26 (Tom Riles);
  11 (Joe Robbins); 21, 26 (Brian Spurlock)
AP/Wide World: 7, 9, 10, 14, 18, 23, 25

Book production by Shoreline Publishing Group, LLC
Art direction and design by The Design Lab

Library of Congress Cataloging-in-Publication Data

Gigliotti, Jim.
  Jeff Gordon : simply the best / by Jim Gigliotti.
      p. cm. — (The world of NASCAR series)
Summary: A simple biography of NASCAR championship driver, Jeff Gordon. Includes biblio-
graphical references and index.
  ISBN 1-59187-007-0 (lib. bdg. : alk. paper)
  1. Gordon, Jeff, 1971– —Juvenile literature. 2. Automobile racing drivers—United States—
Biography—Juvenile literature. [1. Gordon, Jeff, 1971– 2. Automobile racing drivers.] I. Title.
II. Series.
  GV1032.G67 G55 2002
  796.72'06—dc21   2002004646

J E F F   G O R D O N

Table of Contents

I N T R O D U C T I O N

Focused—and Fast!

When it's 90° Fahrenheit (32° Celsius) outside his car and 140° Fahrenheit (60° Celsius) inside it, Jeff Gordon keeps his cool. When he is going nearly 200 miles per hour (333 kilometers per hour), he slows down the action in his mind. When the engine's roar is surpassed only by the crowd's roar, Jeff's concentration is intense. When he waits for just the right time to pass the leader and win, he is at his best.

Jeff is arguably the most popular and certainly the most successful NASCAR driver. NASCAR stands for the National Association for **Stock Car** Automobile Racing circuit. Its

Jeff Gordon is NASCAR's most successful driver.

Winston Cup races are the highest level of stock car racing. In November 2001, Jeff won his fourth NASCAR championship. He was the best driver over the course of the entire season. Only two drivers in NASCAR history have ever won more titles.

Along with being a great driver, Jeff is a fan favorite. It's not just his on-track success that makes Jeff so popular. Whether meeting with fans, the **media,** or his crew, Jeff is humble and gracious. He is articulate and sincere, and has a genuine affection for a sport that has been central to his life— almost from the very beginning.

Jeff drives a Chevrolet Monte Carlo sponsored by DuPont, a paint company.

C H A P T E R   O N E

Born To Be a Racer

T he first time Jeff Gordon got in a race car, he knew that driving would be his destiny. "I was fascinated by it," he said. Jeff was only four years old, and the vehicle was a miniature racer. He quickly figured out how to make the car start and stop, and go fast and slow. Mostly, he went fast. He was hooked from the start. A life-long passion had begun. "I knew I wanted to be a race car driver," he says.

So his mother and stepfather bought him a 6-foot (2-meter) quarter-midget race car. **Quarter-midgets** are small motorized cars built low to the ground. By the time he was five, Jeff was competing in events in his hometown of Vallejo, California. Immediately, he began winning.

Jeff was eight when he became a national champion in the quarter-midgets. He was only nine when he moved up to

go-karts, which are slightly larger cars. When he was just 13, he graduated to **sprint cars.** He was almost always racing against kids older than he was, and he was almost always winning. "All my life, I've been pushed to do things at a young age. Most of those things nobody else had ever done before,"

Fathers and sons often work together to build and race quarter-midget cars.

Jeff says. "I was always one step ahead of the other guys as far as age."

He was always one step ahead on the racetrack, too. It quickly became obvious that he had a special talent for driving. Northern California, however, is not exactly a hotbed for racing activity. So his parents sold their home and moved to Pittsboro, Indiana, when Jeff was 14.

Pittsboro offered Jeff more opportunities for racing. The local age requirements were different from those in California. He could race bigger cars at a younger age. Indiana also was in the heart of **Indy-car** country, not far from the Indianapolis Motor Speedway. Indy cars are full-size race cars. Unlike stock cars, they have long, tubular bodies. They have no fenders, so they're known as **open-wheel** cars.

The annual Indy 500 is one of the world's most famous races. Jeff grew up idolizing Indy 500 winners. "We went to the track the day after the Indy 500 one year. We toured the museum and took the bus tour," Jeff says. "I thought it was

The famous Indianapolis Motor Speedway is the home of the Indy 500 race.

the greatest thing! We saw where the cars actually ran and where they were went for pit stops."

Most people assumed that Jeff would become an Indy-car driver. Even Jeff figured that's where his future would lead. His career path, however, would not take him to those open-wheeled cars, though. Instead, he got into the driver's seat of a stock car for the first time when he was 19. The car was different from anything he had raced before. Nevertheless, he

Four-time Indy 500 champ A. J. Foyt was one of Jeff Gordon's heroes.

THE BRICKYARD 400

In 1980, Jeff Gordon was only nine years old and still living in California. That year, he visited the Indianapolis Motor Speedway for the first time. Later, he was a teenager in Indiana when he would drive by the track and picture himself taking the checkered flag. "I dreamed as a kid to be like A. J. Foyt and Rick Mears and Bobby Unser and Al Unser," Jeff says. Those were all famous Indy car drivers.

"I never dreamed it would be in a stock car."

Stock cars, in fact, didn't even race at the storied Indianapolis track until 1994. That year, NASCAR's Brickyard 400 (right) was held for the first time. Jeff won the race. "The Daytona 500 is our biggest event," he says. "But I don't know if any win will ever top that first Brickyard 400. I'd have to say that was the all-time win for me."

had the same feeling of destiny he got from that miniature car when he was a little kid. "Once I drove a stock car I knew it, then and there," Jeff says. "I knew that this was the kind of car I wanted to drive for the rest of my career."

In 1994, Jeff and his crew "kissed the bricks" at Indy after Jeff won the Brickyard 400.

C H A P T E R   T W O

Off to a Fast Start

Like everything else in his racing career, Jeff Gordon got off to a fast start in stock cars. He became a pro racer less than one year after he first drove a stock car. His first stop was driving on NASCAR's Busch Series circuit. The Busch Series is just a step below the Winston Cup Series. It's like the highest minor leagues in pro baseball. Busch Series cars weigh slightly less and are not as powerful as Winston Cup cars.

Jeff was 20 when he earned the Busch Series rookie of the year award in 1991. The next year, he got his first start in a Winston Cup race. Early in 1993, he became the youngest driver to win a 125-mile (201-kilometer) qualifying race before the Daytona 500.

The Daytona 500 is the most important and prestigious event on the NASCAR schedule. Jeff didn't win the race that year. He finished fifth. The qualifying victory, however, proved that he could race successfully on the storied track. It also proved that he could beat the best drivers in the world.

"In my wildest dreams, I never would have guessed this would happen," Jeff said after winning the qualifying race. That victory and a fine season helped him win the 1993 rookie of the year award.

Jeff's first official Winston Cup win came at the 1994

Who's the guy with the mustache? It's Jeff as a young Winston Cup driver.

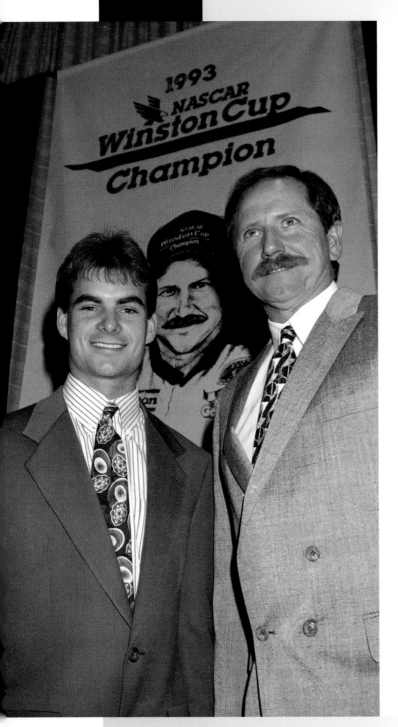

Coca-Cola 600 in Concord, North Carolina. It was a dramatic victory. The 22-year-old outwitted his older and more experienced foes. He was in third place, 20 laps from the finish, when most of the leaders went in to their final pit stop for four tires and gas. When Jeff and his team saw that, they took on only two tires and gas. It meant that Jeff's stop was faster than the other drivers' stops. He left the pits in first place. Soon after, he held on for an emotional victory.

As the 1993 Rookie of the Year, Jeff posed with NASCAR champion Dale Earnhardt.

"The [checkered] flag came out and I completely lost it," he said. "There were tears running down my face."

On the track, Jeff was rising rapidly in respect and fame among his fellow drivers and among fans. Off the track, his appeal to men and women of all ages helped increase NASCAR's popularity. Jeff and other drivers such as Dale Earnhardt helped the sport achieve amazing growth in the 1990s. "I'm really proud to be part of it," Jeff says.

HOME LIFE

When Jeff was a young driver, veteran drivers often helped him out. Today, as a successful driver himself, he is returning the favor. Beginning in 2002, Jeff was not only a driver, he was an owner. With Rick Hendrick, Jeff owns the car driven by rookie Jimmie Johnson. Jeff chose Jimmie to drive based on Jimmie's success in Busch racing.

At the 2002 Daytona 500, Jimmie proved that Jeff had made the right choice. Jimmie grabbed the pole position. It was one of only a few times a rookie had done that. He celebrated with Jeff (above) after clinching that key spot. Will Jeff be as successful as an owner as he is as a driver? That's up to Jimmie Johnson.

CHAPTER   THREE

The Thinking Man's Driver

B y 1995, Jeff Gordon had ascended to the top of his profession. He won seven races. At 24 years old, he became the youngest Winston Cup champion of the modern era. Dale Earnhardt was one of Jeff's rivals. Dale was 20 years older than Jeff. The older driver said Jeff would probably celebrate with a glass of milk. He wasn't laughing when he said it.

Earnhardt may have been referring to Jeff's young age or to his squeaky-clean image. Either way, Jeff played along. When he was named champion at the awards dinner, he brought out a bucket filled with ice. Jeff pulled a glass out of the bucket, which normally held champagne. Jeff toasted his competitors—and the glass was filled with milk, of course.

It's a good thing Jeff had learned to roll with the punches.
His sudden and dazzling success often bred resentment. He
was, after all, only in his mid-20s. He also seemed to have it
all. He had fame, fortune, and a beautiful wife—even a
Winston Cup championship.

**The champ! Jeff celebrates after winning his first
Winston Cup title in 1995.**

Jeff and longtime crew chief Ray Evernham won three titles together.

Some fans and fellow drivers suggested that Jeff's racing success had more to do with his situation than his driving. They hinted that with the same car and crew, almost anyone could have done as well.

There's no doubt that Jeff's crew is one reason for his fantastic racing record. In fact, Jeff is quick to give his team credit after every victory. There's a lot more to it than a capable crew, however. When Jeff is in the driver's seat, he sees the race unfold like no one else.

"Jeff has a different sense of time than you and I," Ray Evernham told *Time* magazine. Evernham was Jeff's **crew chief** from 1993–1999. "He can slow down the race in his mind. He can see things coming around and react before the next guy."

Jeff also talks of feeling like he's moving in slow motion during a race. That is, his mind is working faster than the action is moving around him. Former NFL quarterback Joe Montana and basketball star Michael Jordan have said similar

things. It's a gift that only the greatest athletes seem to have.

"When it comes down to separating a good race car driver from a great race car driver, it has to do with thinking fast," Jeff said on CNN. "It takes someone who can use his head. He has to know when to be patient and when to be aggressive. A lot of thinking goes on in that race car. To me, a smart race car driver is a great race car driver.

"If you've gotten to NASCAR, you've got the skills, you've got the talent. When it comes to winning or losing, I think it's the driver who really uses his head."

Moments before a race, Jeff prepares himself for one thing: winning.

RACING IS A TEAM SPORT

Jeff Gordon's crew is known as the "Rainbow Warriors" because of their multi-colored cars and uniforms. Like every NASCAR driver, Jeff knows that much of his success depends on his crew. That is especially true during the race along pit road.

In a pit stop, seven crew members are allowed "over the wall" to service the car. Obviously, the faster the pit stops, the greater the chances of winning the race.

The over-the-wall gang is responsible for fueling the car and changing the tires. A gas-can man and catch-can man fuel the car in the back. A jack man, two tire carriers, and two tire-changers replace the wheels. As many as a dozen other people work "behind the wall" to make sure Gordon's car is performing its best.

Like everything else about NASCAR, the pit crew's work has to be done fast. A team should change four tires and fill a car with gas in less than 20 seconds!

C H A P T E R   F O U R

From Wonder Boy to Man of the Year

By the time he was 27, Jeff Gordon had won three Winston Cup championships. They came in 1995, 1997, and 1998. That kind of domination earned him the nickname "Wonder Boy." Soon, however, the boy would grow up to be his own man.

Crew chief Ray Evernham left the team late in the 1999 season to form his own team. He asked Jeff to come along, but Jeff declined out of loyalty to car owner Rick Hendrick. Jeff seized the opportunity to prove that he could still win without Evernham, his friend and mentor.

It was a bit rocky at first. In 2000, with a whole new crew, Jeff slipped to ninth place in the standings. That's still a pret-

Jeff jumps for joy after winning a race in Atlanta. The victory clinched his 1997 Winston Cup crown.

ty good year for most drivers, but it was Jeff's lowest finish since his rookie season. Critics wondered if his winning days were through. That didn't bother Jeff, though. "What I like about the criticism is that it motivates me and this team to go out and prove them wrong," Jeff says.

So Jeff set out to do just that. "We had to rebuild and come together as basically a new team," he says. "We had to climb the mountain again."

He had lots of support from his team. "Jeff makes you want to do a better job," says Robbie Loomis, who took over as crew chief. "His ability and his heart, the way he treats people, all make you want to do the very best job possible."

Robbie Loomis took over as Jeff's crew chief in 2000. Together, they won it all in 2001.

They did the best job possible in 2001. That year, Jeff won six races and earned seven **pole positions.** He finished among the top 10 in 24 of 36 races. In the end, he easily beat the competition to win his fourth Winston Cup title. "There were some tough times," Jeff said after clinching the championship. "To see these guys stick together and come back this year makes me really proud."

Jeff's fourth title put him in some **elite** company. Only legendary racers Richard Petty and Dale Earnhardt ever won more Winston Cup titles than Jeff has. Petty and Earnhardt

Jeff's DuPont car leads the way from the pole position, one of seven he earned in 2001.

Jeff sprays his crew with champagne after winning
his fourth Winston Cup title in 2001.

each won a NASCAR-record seven championships. Jeff, how-ever, is the first to win four by age 30. "Winning four champi-onships is mind-boggling," Jeff says. "It's going to take time to sink in."

On top of it all, Jeff was named NASCAR's True Value man of the year in 2001. That award was given for his involve-ment in civic and charitable activities. "I have been so blessed to have the chance to give back," he says. He helps children who are struggling with illness and families in need through the Jeff Gordon Foundation.

The foundation is in keeping with Jeff's character. He is universally recognized as one of the NASCAR circuit's good guys.

"Nobody's perfect," team owner Rick Hendrick once told *Sports Illustrated*. "But I'll tell you what. Jeff Gordon is about as near perfect as you can get."

HOW TO WIN THE CUP

The Winston Cup championship is earned by accumulating the most points in NASCAR's grueling 36-race schedule each year. Points are awarded for the place that a driver finishes in a given race and for leading any laps.

Every time a driver wins a race, he earns 175 points. Second place gets 170, third place 165, and fourth place 160. The points go down from there for every place in the race. Any driver who leads a lap earns another five points. The driver who leads the most laps in a race gets five more on top of that.

Jeff Gordon won six races in the 2001 season, and at some point led in 25 of the 36 races. He led the most laps 11 times. He ended with a total of 5,112 points. As you can see, those points add up fast!

When you win four Winston Cup titles, good things happen. In 2002, Jeff took part in the Winter Olympics torch run.

JEFF GORDON'S LIFE

1971   Born on August 4 in Vallejo, California

1986   Jeff's family moves to Pittsboro, Indiana, in the heart of Indy-car country

1991   Named NASCAR's Busch Series rookie of the year

1992   Gets his first start in a Winston Cup race in the season finale in Atlanta

1993   Earns Winston Cup rookie-of-the-year honors

1994   Earns his first Winston Cup victory at the Coca-Cola 600 in Charlotte

1994   Wins the inaugural Brickyard 400 at the famed Indianapolis Motor Speedway, near his Indiana home

1994   Marries Brooke Sealey, a former Miss Winston model

1995   Becomes the youngest Winston Cup champion of the modern era

1997   Becomes the youngest driver ever to win the famous Daytona 500

1997   Wins his second Winston Cup championship

1998   Wins 13 races on the way to his second consecutive Winston Cup title, his third championship overall

2000   Takes the checkered flag at the DieHard 500 to become the youngest driver to win 50 career races

2001   Joins legendary stars Richard Petty and Dale Earnhardt as the only four-time Winston Cup champions

GLOSSARY

crew chief—the "coach" of the race team, and the person responsible for keeping things running smoothly before and during a race

drafting—When a car follows another car very closely, the front car reduces wind resistance on the back car. The back car can use less energy (above).

elite—the highest level; a select few of the top in any profession

go-karts—small, open, four-wheel racers with gasoline engines

Indy cars—an open-wheel, open-cockpit race car

media—the Internet, magazines, newspapers, television, and radio personnel who report NASCAR news

open-wheel—a car without fenders whose tires are visible all the way around

pole positions—the fastest driver in qualifying trials starts the race at this best position, which is the inside spot on the front row

quarter-midget—a six-foot, open-wheel race car with a single-cylinder engine and full suspension

sprint cars—single-seat, front-engine racers for short tracks

stock car—a standard automobile style specially modified for racing

When drafting, a driver (above, No. 99) follows only inches away from another car at very high speed.

FOR MORE INFORMATION ABOUT JEFF GORDON

Books

Center, Bill. *Ultimate Stock Car.* New York: DK Publishing, 2000

Christopher, Matt. *Jeff Gordon.* New York: Little Brown & Co., 2001.

Dougherty, Teri. *Jeff Gordon.* Minneapolis: Abdo & Daughters, 2000.

Ethan, Eric. *Daytona 500.* Milwaukee: Gareth Stevens, 1999.

Sherman, Josepha. *Jeff Gordon.* Crystal Lake, Ill.: Heinemann Library, 2001.

Stewart, Mark. *Jeff Gordon: Rainbow Warrior.* Brookfield, Conn.: Millbrook Press, 2000.

Web Sites

Jeff Gordon's Official Site
http://www.jeffgordon.com
To read the personal messages that Jeff posts to fans, along with news of his racing career and the work of his Foundation

The Official Web Site of NASCAR
http://www.nascar.com
For an overview of an entire season of NASCAR as well as the history of the sport and a dictionary of racing terms

Fox Sports Network
http://www.foxsports.com
Click on the checkered flag, then NASCAR to find more details about every NASCAR race

INDEX

ABOUT THE AUTHOR

Jim Gigliotti is a freelance writer who lives with his wife and two young children in Oak Park, California. He has worked for the University of Southern California athletic department, the Los Angeles Dodgers, and the National Football League.